Glenn Family

Puppy Love

Puppy Love

TEVVY BALL

ARIEL BOOKS

ANDREWS AND MCMEEL

KANSAS CITY

ISBN: 0-8362-2651-8
Library of Congress Catalog Card Number: 96-85921

Contents

Puppy Love

Introduction

In mid-January, 1953, when my mother was eight and a half months pregnant, my father was working at the United Nations in New York, writing and producing a radio newscast that aired each night at ten o'clock. One bitterly cold day, he suddenly decided that the child due two weeks hence would be preceded by a puppy. He went out on his lunch break, and, as luck would have it,

found a pet store nearby on Forty-second Street. In the window was a tiny cocker pup about six weeks old. My dad went into the store and bought him, put him in a shoe box, and went back to work.

As he wrote the script for that

night's broadcast, representatives of various countries stopped by to put their particular spin on the day's events as they did every afternoon; this afternoon, they ceased their wrangling long enough to coo a bit over the hopelessly adorable little puppy with big brown eyes and floppy ears peering out of the shoe box on the floor.

The broadcast complete, my father gathered the box and its precious cargo under his Burberry's overcoat of woolen tweed and headed out through a driving snowstorm to catch the eleven o'clock train for the northern suburb of

Hartsdale. My mother, who had no idea that a cocker puppy was also on the way, was waiting for him at the station with the Pontiac they had recently bought for eighty dollars. The train pulled in, and then my dad got down and hurried into the waiting car. He quickly pulled the small shoe box from under his coat, and, although he had no proof that the upcoming child would be a boy, announced to his amazed wife, "My son shall have a dog."

This tiny cocker, whom my parents named Michael, was the first of three puppies who would inscribe themselves into our family's affections. The second, an adorably timid little collie we named Kyrie, followed about ten years later, appearing one Christmas morning a few months after Michael had died. She was followed in turn by another cocker puppy, Cappuccino, whom my parents picked up about the

time that their children were
starting to leave the family nest.

The circumstances,
of course, were
different   for
each, because

puppies enter families in many different ways. Perhaps there are children, actual or imminent, in need of a friend. Perhaps there's a house that's beginning to seem empty. Perhaps, after long reflection and careful study, we arrive at the conclusion that a new pup is *de rigueur*. Or perhaps the truth appears in a flash of revelation, high up in a skyscraper overlooking New York City. In that moment, the next ten years suddenly come into focus; we see into the future, and we know that in some way it must include a canine companion.

The story of Michael's arrival became part of family legend, recounted with gusto many times over the following years. From the snowy station, my parents headed for home, a Victorian house with three stories and a basement heated by a single temperamental furnace. Arriving sometime after midnight, they both suddenly realized that the puppy might catch cold, were he left to his own devices in the vast, drafty house. So they both settled in the parlor, one of our warmer rooms, and stayed up with the little fellow all night long in order to keep him warm. Two weeks later my parents and their puppy got back into the Pontiac and drove through another blizzard to a hospital in Brooklyn, where, within a few hours, I followed Michael into the family.

To Pick a Puppy

During that first winter, my parents quickly learned what every would-be puppy owner finds out: taking a young puppy home is the kind of commitment that can seriously complicate your life. And it goes without saying

that not all pups are right for all lives.

The American Kennel Club currently lists 145 different breeds of dogs—and, therefore, of puppies. They vary widely in size and personality, from tiny Chihuahuas to gigantic Saint Bernards, from toy poodles to sleek greyhounds. Dog breeds are divided into seven groups: sporting dogs, hounds, working dogs, terriers, toys, nonsporting dogs, and herding dogs. There is also a "miscellaneous class," which consists largely of breeds still awaiting official classification. The behavioral characteristics of any given pup will depend on various factors such as breed, early handling, and so on.

Since puppies play an important—not to say intrusive—role in our lives, it's a good idea to make every attempt to select the puppy that's just right for you. If you live in a small city apartment, for example, you might be better off opting for a smaller and more sedate dog, while a house with a fenced yard or a rural home with plenty of room to roam is usually better for a larger, active breed. If you're looking for a lovable lap-sitting dog, you might select a different breed from someone who has a

watchdog in mind; in the latter case a territorial pooch, such as some kind of terrier, might well be the order of the day. Terriers come in a variety of breeds, from the flighty Airedale to the tenacious Staffordshire bull terrier. Originally bred to hunt rodents, they tend to be spunky, independent, and territorial, and they love to bark at the smallest provocation.

On the other hand, if you are seeking a jogging mate, you might want an active, athletic dog that can also benefit from plenty of regular exercise—perhaps a collie, German shepherd, or

Shetland sheepdog. Not surprisingly, they tend to be a bit less territorial than little pooches (who are, I suspect, eternally trying to overcome an inferiority complex). Widely considered among the most intelligent breeds, herders make active and affectionate pets, as do many of the "worker" dogs, such as huskies and malamutes.

When I was in college, a friend of mine, Cindy, who was a real exercise nut, got herself a little husky pup to accompany her on her afternoon jog around campus. A graduate student in philosophy, she named her pup Niet-

zsche, after the noted German thinker. Quite likely following in the footsteps of his namesake, Nietzsche early on exhibited an independent, even unruly, nature; he would often ramble off on his own, leaving Cindy to wander the halls of the philosophy department, calling out her puppy's name. Everyone in the department soon got used to this recurring little drama, and thought nothing more of it.

One afternoon at the beginning of winter term, however, a visiting professor who had just arrived at the school was astonished to find the tranquillity of his office hour shattered by a woman's voice calling out, "Nietzsche, where are you?" He poked his head out into the hall, only to be confronted by the sight of a very attractive young woman who, by all appearances, had completely lost her mind.

Well acquainted with the eccentricities of graduate students, he did not wish to cause undue embarrassment to this poor creature. She was obviously

much loved by her colleagues, he sur-
mised, in the way that villagers once
shared a general affection for the town
idiot, so he quietly withdrew into his
office and closed the door.

At that very moment, however, the
frisky pup appeared from around the
corner, and Cindy loudly exclaimed in
relief, "Oh, Nietzsche, there you are."
This was too much for the good professor; wide-eyed, he opened his door
again, with what could be called a blend
of incredulity and irritation. Upon see-
ing Cindy and her playful pup, of
course, the mystery was solved.

Puppies come in all sizes. I recently went to visit a friend of mine who had acquired a Saint Bernard about six months earlier, and there I discovered the biggest puppy I had ever seen. It must have weighed a hundred pounds, but it still seemed to frolic like a kid; to accommodate it, my friend finally had to find a house with a bigger yard. In spite of its size, by the way, the Saint Bernard is usually very gentle with children and will make an excellent family pet.

Perhaps because of my early acquaintance with Michael, the sporting dogs—pointers, spaniels, setters, and retrievers—originally bred to help hunters flush and retrieve birds, have always held a special place in my heart. Our second cocker spaniel, Cappuccino, was quite a bit friskier than Michael; we came to the perhaps

unwarranted conclusion that he was rather frustrated at not being able to exercise the honorable profession of his ancestors. He may also have been a would-be guard dog, a legend in his own mind, who felt foiled over never testing his mettle against a potentially dangerous intruder—a disappointment which, I must admit, I was never quite able to share.

In any case, as a little pup, Cappy was fascinated by birds; we would often find ourselves sitting on the front porch when a crow would alight on the lawn not far away. Cappy would scramble down the steps, and, in a streak of brown, bolt for the bird, barking at the top of his lungs. The crow, of course, would lift with mocking ease into the nearest tree, while Cappy would trot back toward the porch, head high and beaming with pride as if he had just driven away a burglar.

One of the Family

While a new kitten, however playful, can usually be accommodated with a little patience and goodwill, a peppy young puppy can seem to remake a household in its own image. In many ways, a puppy is a

labor of love, work that repays hand-somely as you fashion a loyal friend who will lend joy and warmth to your lives for many years to come.

When you first bring the little fellow home, it's a good idea to have on hand a few essential items—food and water bowls, a couple of rawhide chew bones, the same puppy food that the breeder or pet store was using, and, of course, a few weeks' supply of old newspapers. Set aside an area—preferably uncarpeted, such as a kitchen or bathroom— as his primary living space. Make sure that there's nothing sharp or electrical lying around, put down plenty of newspapers, and enclose the area with a puppy gate. This gate is perhaps your most important purchase; sturdy and flexible, it allows the puppy to be safely kept without feeling cut off from the rest of the family.

During the first days, be sure to give your new friend plenty of playful, loving attention. Be careful, however, not to overwhelm him. You should be kind but also firm; remember, you are training puppy, puppy isn't training you. Of course, you'll need to modify your behavior according to your puppy's personality. If the little guy is too aggressive, you'll need to teach him to recognize your authority. But if he's overly shy, you'll need to be very, very gentle, to make certain that this initial timidity doesn't develop into a lifelong neurosis.

And no matter what ingenious ways your new companion finds to tug on your heartstrings, you'll have to resist the urge to sweep him up in your arms every time he starts to whine. The pup will outgrow this initial loneliness—usually in a few days. If your pooch starts getting the idea that he can bend you to his bidding by uttering an occasional whimper, you will have a miniature monster who will prove quite troublesome indeed.

In general, it's a good idea to avoid setting up too rigid a routine. A friend of mine, for example, who had recently acquired a little Samoyed, inaugurated their relationship by taking the pup for a walk each morning, precisely at seven o'clock. For a while, pup and owner got along fine, but when my friend decided to sleep in one Sunday morning a few months later, the two encountered their first crisis. The poor pup went nearly wild with anxiety, howling at the bedroom door until my friend dragged herself from bed. Although things were finally resolved to everyone's satisfaction, both owner and pup would have been only too happy to have avoided the whole experience.

In a similar vein, there are times
when puppies have to be protected

from themselves. Cappuccino, for in-
stance, quickly developed the habit of
yapping at anyone's heels; one night, in
the dark, he had the misfortune to catch
the heel of my father's sock just as my
dad was lifting his foot. Cappy was raised
off the ground and his little jaw was
broken; we had to feed him baby food
for several months until he recovered.

By the way, if you are going to be
bringing your puppy into a household
where an older dog already lives, it's a
good idea to conduct the introductions
on neutral territory—say, a nearby park.
This way the older dog can sniff around

the newcomer without feeling that its home territory is being invaded by a stranger. In turn, the new pup will most likely feel less frightened. When you do take puppy home, be sure to provide him with his own toys, chewing bone, and so forth.

After an initial period of adaptation, you'll likely find that the two get on at least tolerably well. And if your dog has been feeling lonely and depressed, the presence of a young pup can actually improve his general outlook. It's a better solution than Prozac, which some dog owners have actually tried on particularly gloomy pets, apparently with varying degrees of success.

Having a puppy around can also do wonders for humans. In 1860, no less an authority than Florence Nightingale commented that having a pooch around is good for whatever

ails you. More recently, it has been shown that the simple act of petting your pooch lowers blood pressure and heart rate, thereby significantly lessening the risk of cardiovascular disease. It can also ease depression. Another recent study suggests that a puppy can help save a troubled marriage, as well as add luster to a happy love.

The Ties That Bond

Many people believe that dogs are psychic, developing their powers in the early, formative months of puppyhood. One friend of mine reports that her little Labrador retriever, after only a few months in the house, would start wagging his tail in joyous anticipation some ten or fifteen minutes before her husband would come home. She insists that this always happened long before there were any sounds for the dog to pick up on. As far as I'm concerned, the jury is still out on that one. . . .

Much is made also of the special bond that canines and humans can share. I experienced something of this sort with our first dog, Michael. When my parents first brought me home as an infant from the hospital, Michael became very attached to me; my mother would sit in the drafty Victorian's one

warm room, working on the book that she was writing; I'd lie in the colonial-style cradle my dad had fashioned; and Michael would pace back and forth between us. Puppy and baby grew up together. Michael, I have been told, seemed to identify with this funny-looking infant; he fancied himself my guardian, at times standing on his hind legs and looking down into the crib, as if he were checking on my progress.

Of course, I have no conscious memories of that first winter. Nor can I remember the house; when I was five months old, we moved to another dwelling, which we also inhabited briefly, and which I have also forgotten. What I do possess is a few old photographs: of myself in the crib, with Michael on the floor nearby; of the yard, blanketed in snow, with the towering Victorian discernible in the background through bare, frost-clad trees; of my father and me, some three months later, on a day warm enough for him to be shirtless, the yard now free of snow and in budding leaf; and, apparently taken on the same day, a picture of my dad peering straight at the camera, holding a cocker pup in his arms.

Our family's two other dogs, Kyrie and Cappuccino, were both well loved in their time. But now, so many years later, the circumstances of their arrival as pups seem to have faded, while Michael's early days with the family have, if anything, grown in stature. Perhaps it is because the guileless floppy-eared pup, so vulnerable in that bitter January night of long ago, embodied

the hopes my parents had for the family they had set about creating, hopes which, as the years passed, and in spite of misfortunes inevitable or otherwise, would indeed come to such joyous fruition.

Kyrie was more my sisters' dog, while Cappuccino belonged especially to my parents. Michael, though, was always first and foremost my dog; perhaps a bond was formed during that initial winter, when he would get up on his hind legs and peer down into the crib where I lay. Perhaps he recognized—perhaps we both recognized—

that, as newcomers in a strange and mysterious world, we had something in common.

With the passage of time, our relationship proved expansive enough to include my sisters as well; every evening for years, as our family settled into sleep, Michael, before curling up at the foot of my bed, would make his nocturnal rounds, poking his head into each of our rooms, as if to ensure that, for the moment at least, everything was as it s h o u l d be.

Puppy Patter

A dog is like an eternal Peter Pan, a child who never grows old and who therefore is always available to love and be loved.

—AARON KATCHER

When a puppy takes fifty catnaps in the course of the day, he cannot always be expected to sleep the night through. It is too much to ask.

—ALBERT PAYSON TERHUNE

Children and dogs are as necessary to the welfare of the country as Wall Street and the railroads.

—HARRY S. TRUMAN

Buy a pup and your money
   will buy
Love unflinching that cannot lie.

—RUDYARD KIPLING

The prospective buyer sits in the middle of the litter and plays with all the pups. The one that pulls at his cuff, pounces through the pack, climbs up into his lap, and paws at his shirt to give him a love lick is usually the one that wins his heart and gets bed and board for life.

—RICHARD A. WOLTERS

Happiness is a warm puppy.
—CHARLES SCHULZ

For though he had very little Latin beyond "Cave canem," he had, as a young dog, devoured Shakespeare (in a tasty leather binding).

—DODIE SMITH

His puppyhood was a period of foolish rebellion. He was always worsted, but he fought back because it was his nature to fight back. And he was unconquerable.

—JACK LONDON

The best way to get a puppy is to beg for a baby brother—and they'll settle for a puppy every time.

—WINSTON PENDELTON

Dogs, like human infants, learn by imitation. Show him what you want; whether or not he performs, he will be duly amused by your hilarious attempts to please him.

—STEPHEN BAKER

My little dog—a heartbeat at my feet.

—EDITH WHARTON

There is no psychiatrist in the
world like a puppy licking your face.

—BERN WILLIAMS

I cannot impress on my readers too strongly the necessity to be firm but kind to a puppy. His idea of your authority is forming, and if he knows you give in on the slightest whimper, you are whacked for life.

—BARBARA WOODHOUSE

Being patted is what it is all about.

—ROGER CARAS

The text was set in Bembo
and the display in Party Plain
at Snap-Haus Graphics of
Edgewater, N.J.

The spot art is from Art Parts and
Object Gear.

Book design by
Diane Stevenson